A BEGINNER'S GUIDE TO GOD

(And We're *All* Beginners)

ERIC NEAL

iUniverse, Inc.
Bloomington

A Beginner's Guide to God
(And We're *All* Beginners)

iUniverse books may be ordered through booksellers or by contacting:

iUniverse
1663 Liberty Drive
Bloomington, IN 47403
www.iuniverse.com
1-800-Authors (1-800-288-4677)

ISBN: 978-1-4759-4847-9 (sc)
ISBN: 978-1-4759-4849-3 (e)

Library of Congress Control Number: 2012917903

Printed in the United States of America

iUniverse rev. date: 12/11/2012

This book is dedicated to all those children who have lost their lives or are suffering as a result of mankind's intolerance to fellow humans.

It is okay to have different beliefs. We don't need to fight because of it. We are all the product of one Creator, who clearly does not approve of the senseless animosity toward other members of the human family.

We owe it to our children to stop the stupidity and allow them to enjoy the good things this life has to offer, such as a peaceful and loving environment.

It is hoped that leaders and citizens of war-torn countries will recognize the vital importance of focusing on those things that unite rather than divide us and secure a safer future for our children.

Contents

PREFACE

Having been born into a Christian environment and having attended Sunday school, I accepted Christ but felt confused by the number of different religions. The Christian teachings about false prophets made me reluctant to consider other religions, but once I conquered that barrier, I started to investigate. Although I found the teachings of other religions full of valuable guidance, to me they were just like Christianity with a different cultural flavor. Then, at the age of twenty six, I was introduced to the Baha'i faith, and it was like finding the missing piece of the jigsaw puzzle. The first chapter of my search was complete, and a new and more exciting chapter was just beginning.

The research I have done for this book has reinforced for me the unity of religion. In studying the various religions you do find some contradictions, but the overwhelming feeling gained from studying the religions with an open mind is an amazing sense of attraction to all the religions. This created in me a strong bond with all the prophets, and this has cemented my unshakable belief in the reality of progressive revelation. A strong belief in any one of the religions and its founder is so understandable when you read the teachings, but I find to open one's mind to the big picture brings about a strong sense of love for the whole of humanity.

It is interesting to observe how the focus of each religion has progressively evolved to meet the changing conditions in the status of society. The earlier religious teachings focused very much on the individual, whereas the latter prophets provided guidance for relationships, then for tribal unity and national unity, and now for world unity through the teachings of Baha'u'llah.

I encourage everyone to study the history and teachings of some of the world's major religions. Our history books focus on the wars, yet it is the spiritual teachings of God's messengers that have really shaped history and have provided the catalyst for the positive and glorious future toward which mankind is headed.

A Beginner's Guide to God is just that—a guide. Nobody after reading it will become an expert on the subject. With the exception of the prophets, who undoubtedly were blessed with special knowledge and understanding, there have never been any experts, although throughout history there have been many spiritually attuned people whose exemplary lives have provided inspiration and influenced mankind's progress. But if this book sparks an interest in, or clarifies some aspects of, mankind's most important questions, then it has achieved its objective.

It is not logical to believe that God is accessible only to the academics, the scholars, and the philosophers. A good father is a father to all his children, not to just those more knowledgeable ones. He is equally accessible to all his children. Why would God's relationship with His family be any different? Your understanding of God and your relationship with God is therefore as important and as valid as the next person's. Cherish that relationship.

PART 1

THE BIG PICTURE

CHAPTER 1

THE BIG QUESTIONS

What happens to me when I die?

There can be no more important question than this.

We are on this earth for maybe seventy to eighty years—a bit longer in some cases—but unless we have the right combination of good genes, a healthy lifestyle, and a few other things going for us, we're not likely to be around much after we turn one hundred. Nobody has invented a magic potion yet to allow our human bodies to last forever, and it's not likely that this will happen before we leave for good.

So, seeing we won't be around here forever, what happens after that, and how do we find out? This is where our journey begins.

You likely fall into one of three categories:

    a.   believer
    b.   atheist[1]

---

1 Atheist: A follower of the theory or belief that God does not exist.

c. agnostic[2]

Let's look at these three categories and what they mean.

A Believer

If you fall into this category, it means that you believe that there is a higher form of thought than human thought. And by this we don't mean superior beings from another planet, if they exist. Because even if they existed, they would be asking the same question: Is there yet a higher form of thought?

An Atheist

If you fall into this category, you are not likely to be reading this book, unless you have curiosity as to why people might think differently from you. An atheist doesn't believe in a higher thought than human thought, except for the possibility of extraterrestrial beings. This line of thought is understandable. It is a very clinical thought process that won't entertain anything that can't be scientifically proven.

However, let us examine this a bit further. Because we have thought processes, it is assumed that we can figure out anything. But this is not necessarily the case. If there is something that is beyond human comprehension, it is just that—beyond our comprehension.

Look at that table in front of you. Okay, so maybe there isn't a table, but just pretend there is. Yes, we have the ability to imagine something that we know exists even though we may struggle to imagine something that we haven't seen in some form or another.

Who made that table? A man or maybe a woman? We know that, but does the table know that? Of course not, because the table does not have the capacity to know that and never will.

---

2 Agnostic: A person who is uncertain or non-committal about the existence of God.

What if the power that created the universe is as far above our understanding as the human mind is above that table's understanding? We would never be able to understand that power. So it's a matter of leaving ourselves open to the possibility that such an intelligent power exists. Generally, an atheist would not do that.

An Agnostic

If you are confused as to whether you are a believer or an atheist, then maybe you fall into the agnostic category: you believe in the possibility of some intelligent power beyond our comprehension, but you are not sufficiently convinced to say you are a believer.

This book is really aimed at you.

However, the book is also for believers who need some clarification or additional perspective about what they have learned through various other media.

More Questions

In addition to our initial question—"What happens to me when I die?"—an inquisitive mind would likely wonder about other questions, such as the following:

a. Who or what created the universe?
b. How was it created?
c. Why was it created?
d. Is it really infinite in size?
e. If not, what's at the end of the universe? Empty space? And isn't that also part of the universe?
f. Is some invisible force in control of my life in one way or another?

Will science ever discover the answers to these questions, or do the answers lie outside the realm of human comprehension, regardless of scientific advancement? Maybe the answers lie in the spiritual realm.

What does the spiritual realm mean?

There are many different levels of existence, often referred to as "kingdoms."

There is the mineral kingdom, the plant kingdom, the animal kingdom, and the human kingdom. The inhabitants of each kingdom generally have an appreciation of the kingdoms below their own and make use of the properties of these kingdoms to advance within their own kingdom. For example, humans fully utilize the mineral kingdom (e.g. the properties of soil and water), the plant kingdom (vegetables, fruits, grains, etc.), and the animal kingdom, but the lower kingdoms have little or no understanding of the higher kingdoms. The illustration of the table and its maker is an example of this.

Is the human kingdom the highest level of existence? The purpose of this book is to seriously consider the existence of a higher form of existence, generally referred to as the spiritual kingdom or spiritual realm. As the term infers, it relates to things of the spirit. The *Concise Oxford Dictionary* defines "spirit" as the vital animating essence of a person or the intelligent, non-physical part of a person. This higher kingdom (and there may be more than one) is beyond our comprehension, so the extent to which we recognize the existence of the spiritual kingdom is a matter of faith. The level of such faith often depends upon our study of and reflection on the teachings relating to the many religions that have been revealed to mankind throughout the centuries.

Why do believers believe in a higher power or a higher form of thought? Probably for one or more of the following reasons:

a. They have had some experience in their life that is too amazing to be a sheer coincidence. Such events can happen time and time again, which makes the chance of them being just coincidences an impossibility, leaving people with the feeling that their lives are being led in a certain direction by an external power.

b. They have studied or been exposed to some religious teachings explaining the existence of a higher power, and these teachings have made sense to them.

c. They figure that the things we experience in nature are so amazingly balanced, controlled, and awesome that they couldn't possibly just happen by chance. If that balance wasn't there, human life and, in fact, all forms of life would have become extinct soon after it came into existence. We need the right amount of sunlight, the right amount of heat, the right amount of rain, the process that causes the distribution of water via rain, the right mixture of gases in our atmosphere, and the whole process of regeneration. This balance and these amazing processes have continued for millions, if not billions, of years, along with many other factors necessary for ongoing life. So, if it isn't just a chance in a billion that these conditions continue to sustain us, there must be some thought behind the process.

The watch on your wrist is an example of wonderful human design and engineering. It didn't just all fall into place by chance. How much more wonderful are the things of nature? Surely these could not have just happened by chance either. But what do we know of their creator?

CHAPTER 2

RELIGION

Once you mention the word "God," a person often forms an impression in his or her mind of what God is and then bases his or her belief or disbelief on this perception.

So let's initially focus on that feeling that there may be some amazing power that we can't comprehend, which is the guiding force behind creation. Many people think of this force as "nature," and that is probably as close as we can get to visualizing what this force is, because we can experience the forces of nature all around us. But it falls a long way short of explaining everything, because the question remains: What drives nature?

Throughout history, great spiritual leaders have provided us with insight into these matters. Who are these spiritual leaders, and what motivated them? Here are some of them. (Timeframes for the earlier religions are approximate only.[3])

---

3 The timeframes and dates during which many of the prophets proclaimed their teachings are only approximate because of conflicting theories, so readers may find variations to the dates stated in this book.

Krishna—Introduced the Hindu teachings around 3200 BCE.

Abraham—Introduced the concept of monotheism (one god), probably around 1750 BCE.

Moses—Introduced the Jewish teachings (Judaism) around 1370 BCE.

Zoroaster—Introduced the Zoroastrian teachings around 640 BCE.

Buddha—Introduced the Buddhist teachings around 540 BCE.

Jesus Christ—Introduced the Christian teachings around 27 CE.

Muhammad—Introduced the Islamic teachings around 610 CE.

The Bab—Introduced the Babi teachings from 1844 CE.

Baha'u'llah—Introduced the Baha'i teachings from 1853 CE.

There have been many others, perhaps not so well-known, and we have little in the way of recorded history relating to many of them.

Let us look at what these spiritual leaders have in common.

a. They provided spiritual teachings that have given strong guidance and have been adhered to by large numbers of followers.

b. In many cases strong civilizations have been built based on their teachings.

c. They all refer to a life after the physical life that we are currently experiencing.

d. Their spiritual teachings have been very similar.

Perhaps the best example of the similarity of their teachings is what has become commonly known as the "Golden Rule" regarding how we should treat others. Here are some examples of the various religious teachings on this subject.

Hindu—"This is the sum of duty: do not do to others what would cause pain if done to you" (Mahabharata 5:1517).

Jewish—"What is hateful to you, do not to your fellow man. This is the law: all the rest is commentary" (Talmud, Shabbat 31a; Tobit 4:15).

Buddhism—"Hurt not others in ways that you yourself would find hurtful" (Udana-Varga 5.18).

Christianity—"And as ye would that men should do to you, do ye also to them likewise" (Luke 6:31).

Islam—"None of you (truly) believe until he wishes for his brother what he wishes for himself" (Fourth Hadith of an-Nawawi 13).

Baha'i faith—"Blessed is he who prefereth his brother before himself" (Baha'u'llah, Gleanings, LXVI:8).

What motivated these spiritual leaders to introduce these and other teachings?

If we judge by their own words, they had no choice. Most claim to have been appointed by God and say their teachings come from God.

In part 2 of this book, we look at these religions in more detail.

Why do people tend to follow one religion as opposed to another? Historically, this has been based on where they were born, what was the predominant religion in that country or area, and what religion their parents followed. Regardless of what that religion happened to be, the quality of their teachings, their inspiration, and their moral guidance usually provide no reason to question the validity of their religion, and therefore it is extremely rare that a person would renounce their religion to follow another.

It is more common for people to choose to follow another religion but still believe in the teachings of the religion in which they were raised, seeing no conflict in doing so, as the spiritual teachings of the different religions are very similar.

Chapter 3

Progressive Revelation

When we consider the nature and the similarity of the teachings of each religion, it is not difficult to conclude that they come from the same source.

We have referred to those who have introduced the world's great religions as spiritual leaders; however, they are also referred to by other titles, such as messengers, manifestations, or prophets. The title "manifestations" comes from their claims to be manifestations of God on earth, inasmuch as they are the means by which the guidance or teachings from God is made manifest or clear. They are more commonly referred to as prophets, as much of their teachings are of a prophetic nature. As such, they provide us with an indication of what we can expect in the future. They may also provide prophecies relating to one or more future prophets, often referred to as their own return. In particular, the teachings of Jesus Christ were abundant with such prophecies, and Christians have long speculated on the true meanings of these prophecies and the anticipated return of Christ.

Because of the fact that "prophet" is a more commonly recognized term for these spiritual messengers, we will use that term for the duration of this book, but we hasten to add that prophecy is by no means the most important aspect of their teachings, and that the divine guidance that they have given to their followers is their predominant mission.

We cannot comprehend the reality or power of a "Being" who has the thought processes to create everything we see around us. In fact, we don't even know if they are thought processes, but we can appreciate or expect that this Being whom we call God would want to provide guidance to His creation. Why would He create human beings, with the powers that we have, and not provide us with some insights into the purpose of our existence? To use a modern analogy, it would be like us creating a computer and installing programs without providing any manual or help facilities. So it is logical to expect that He would want to provide us with important guidance.

You will notice that, as in the preceding paragraph, God is usually referred to as "He." We should not get hung up on this. In many languages there is no equivalent of "he" or "she," so in these cases the issue does not exist. We could use the word "It," but that would seem too impersonal.

We need to consider that until recently, let's say just two hundred years ago, the world was a much different place than it is today. Improved means of travel and communication have dramatically changed mankind's thinking and view of the planet. Our thinking, even in the last fifty years, has undergone a massive shift, and it is now easy to see the earth as one global village, despite the multitude of languages and cultures that it comprises. With television and the internet, people are now embracing these differences, seeing them as adding variety and color to our lives.

In the time of Jesus, mankind's understanding and thinking was primitive in comparison to how we think today. There was no comprehension of the size of the planet, the fact that there were people living twelve thousand miles (19,300 km) away, and certainly no comprehension of the variety of different cultures that existed. Had Jesus foretold some of the things we take for granted today, people would not have taken Him seriously. Science needed to advance to enable such developments.

We know that the prophets we have referred to have lived at different times in history and have appeared to different civilizations. The world's population is fragmented, and has therefore resulted in a multitude of different ethnicities and cultures that speak different languages, live in quite different climates, undergo quite different challenges, and develop at very different rates of progress physically, mentally, and scientifically. The guidance required for each civilization has been quite different. Nevertheless, as previously discussed, we find that the spiritual guidance provided was basically the same, probably tempered only by the capacity of the respective peoples to receive and understand it.

An example of where teachings appear to differ would be Moses's teaching of "An eye for an eye and a tooth for a tooth" (Exodus 21:24), whereas twelve hundred years later, Jesus taught, "But I say unto you, That you resist not evil: but whosoever shall smite you on your right cheek, turn to him the other also" (Matthew 5:38). Does this mean that one was right and one was wrong? Not at all. Moses needed to encourage His people to be brave and not be walked over, whereas twelve hundred years later, mankind had progressed to the extent that Jesus could provide an alternative and less aggressive solution. It doesn't mean that Moses was wrong, and in fact the exercising of justice may well require different responses to different situations.

Records show that the whole history of the human race has been permeated by wars and division. In fact, it took until the middle of the twentieth century and the development of a weapon that could destroy millions of people at one time for us to wake up and recognize the potential dangers of continuing to try and resolve disputes by means of armed conflict. Unfortunately, there are still many pockets of the world where fighting continues. How many more lives will be unnecessarily lost in futile armed conflicts before common sense prevails on a global scale?

But we have seen the changing maturity of the human race over the centuries, and more recently we have witnessed in our own lifetimes a change in the determination of most of the governments of the world to collaborate to address serious global issues. The "them and us" syndrome has now been recognized as a huge impediment to mankind's progress.

The closer interaction between the different races, brought about by the internet, improved travel and better détente, has resulted in an increased sharing of religious teachings, whereby we can recognize their similarity. We can therefore open our minds to the possibility that all civilizations have been guided by the same God through a series of prophets. This is one of the fundamental teachings of the Baha'i faith, which refers to the concept as progressive revelation.

Prophets have generally taught that the only path to heaven is through their own teachings, which works against the widespread acceptance of progressive revelation. This has been couched in different terms by different prophets, but nevertheless the inference is the same. Also, they all warned about false prophets—people claiming to be prophets from God when they are not. How do we recognize a false prophet? We can probably find no better guidance on this than by using the measure suggested by Jesus, who said, "Ye shall know them by their fruits" (Matthew 16:12).

We can assume from this that, if those claiming to be prophets bring about positive change for mankind, they should be more favorably considered as valid. Nevertheless, many religious clergy, particularly in Christendom, tend to focus strongly on the dangers of being seduced by false prophets, thereby discouraging people from investigating other religions.

The previous statement may sound somewhat cynical, but it is nevertheless a reality, and opposition to alternative religious thinking, occasionally triggered by religious leaders, is often taken beyond nonacceptance, and followers of other religions are persecuted for their beliefs. But such opposition is finding less and less support as people come to realize that followers of other religions are not bad people.

As a result of this more receptive appreciation of other religions, we are finding that there is now a strong move toward inter-faith activity. While this may not mean acceptance of progressive revelation by all participants, it must surely be a move in the right direction that we can accept that others may have different beliefs and that we can work together toward a common goal, even though we may have some reservations about the validity of the beliefs of others involved in inter-faith activities.

If one accepts the reality of progressive revelation, the teachings of the various religions take on a new meaning, because we then appreciate that the prophets are speaking with one voice. This causes the feeling of exclusiveness to fade, and we recognize the oneness of God and the oneness of religion.

We mentioned earlier that the prophets are so called because much of their teachings revolve around prophecy. We also mentioned that although Jesus could have told us about future developments, this would not have been appropriate. Instead He said, "I have yet many things to say unto you, but ye cannot bear them now. Howbeit when he, the Spirit of truth, is come, he will guide you into all truth" (John 16:12-13). This passage from the Bible and many like it indicate revelations to come, and Christians have speculated for centuries as to the meaning of these prophecies and what is generally referred to as the return of Christ.

Other prophets have made similar prophecies regarding future prophets, and many have also referred to previous prophets, further supporting the reality of progressive revelation. For example, Jesus spoke of Moses, Muhammad spoke of Jesus, and Baha'u'llah spoke with reverence of many of the previous prophets.

The concept of progressive revelation is not complicated. It can be summed up in a few words:

- There is only one God.
- There is basically only one religion—the religion of God—which has been revealed to mankind progressively through a series of prophets chosen by God.
- The teachings of each of the prophets form different chapters of the same all-encompassing religion of God.

Each person should conduct an independent investigation of the truth by studying the teachings of the prophets and not rely on others to tell them what is right and what is wrong. Regardless of which religion we follow, if we took time to become familiar with the teachings of other religions, we would become a much more enlightened and tolerant society.

Chapter 4

Interpretation

To gain a better understanding of God, we must distinguish between the teachings of the prophets, and the churches or other religious institutions that have been built up as a result of those teachings. If we believe in God and His prophets, we would accept that the teachings are from God. However, people have placed their own interpretations on these teachings, and the interpretations have been diverse, resulting in many different sects of the same religion. It is unrealistic to think that one particular sect has been divinely guided, and therefore have gotten it "right," whereas all the others have been wrong. So we must go back to the original teachings with open minds rather than blindly following the interpretation of those who share the teachings with us.

We must bear in mind that many of the early religions were handed down by word of mouth over many centuries. The Christian Bible was compiled some four hundred years after the time of Jesus and is made up from the writings of several Apostles who relied on accounts from numerous sources. So we should take into account that the teachings may have been misreported to some extent.

Depending on who you talk to, you will get a different slant on the accuracy of the Bible's contents. Some will say it is full of contradictions, and some will say that there is not a single contradiction in the Bible and that it's all a matter of how you interpret the various passages.

The reality is that it doesn't matter.

There is only one truth—what actually happened or what actually was said. Whether it is recorded absolutely correctly in the Bible should not be a major factor in our judgment of this holy book. The fact that the Bible was written so long after the event would make one lean toward the belief that it is not 100 percent perfect. The purist may believe that the writing and the compilation of the Bible were divinely inspired and therefore the Bible is perfect, but do we need to concern ourselves with that argument? The important thing is that the Bible is the best account of the life and teachings of Jesus that we have, and whether or not it is word perfect should not be an impediment to using it to decide if we believe that Jesus is who he claims to be or not. Having been exposed to the teachings of Jesus for many decades and experiencing the quality and application of these teachings, my judgment is an unequivocal "yes." But you must make up your own mind based on what you read, what you hear, and what you experience, regardless of which religion you are studying.

CHAPTER 5

THE SPIRITUAL SIDE

This book has attempted to break down some of the barriers that may confuse the searcher after the truth. Much of the book has been written from a logical viewpoint, and the reader may or may not agree with the logic presented. However, there is another side to a belief in God, which is harder to convey on paper or any other media. That is the spiritual side. It is all very well to believe something through logic, but when it comes to believing in God, this is not enough. The natural progression, if you have a belief in God, is to follow His teachings so that we might not only have a better life, but also have more focus, knowing that there is a purpose to life and that we are not here by chance. If this belief does not transform us, it is of no purpose.

How do we become transformed? We have spoken about the power of God and how He is way beyond our understanding, yet the prophets tell us that we can communicate with God through prayer. And what is prayer? It's exactly that: communicating with God.[4] This is often done by groups of people together or individually.

---

4 Prayer: A solemn request or thanksgiving to God.

Usually people find it is more effective to pray in solitude because they can then focus their full attention on the task at hand.

We are told by the prophets that God hears our prayers, and while we may not understand this and the concept of God hearing our prayers may not be an accurate description of the process, most of those who pray feel that they become more enlightened. The whole concept of prayer is something that many people find difficult to comprehend, but we are conditioned to think in terms of time and place and other restrictions, so, it is important that we do not judge what is possible and what is not possible as far as God is concerned. Look at the universe that He has created, and it becomes easier to acknowledge that God has no limitations. As we become more familiar with spiritual teachings, the more we pray, and the more that we become entrenched in our belief, the more spiritually transformed we become.

Barriers to Belief

While on our spiritual journey, there may be many obstacles that we need to overcome in order to affirm our belief. The following are some of them.

Tragedies

When a loved one dies in the prime of life or when a natural disaster occurs, killing hundreds or thousands of innocent people, we ask "Why?" and we find it difficult to understand how a loving God could allow this to happen.

Because this is the only life we know, everything that happens in life has great significance. But if in fact, although our body dies, our soul lives on forever, and therefore our short time on this earth can be compared to the blink of an eye. We sadly reflect on lost lives and suffering, but all these events may be insignificant in the whole scheme of things. Such events may be more to do with the spiritual conditioning of those still living than the ones that have passed on. We really don't know the reasons for these things. Our belief may be challenged, but we can also accept that there is some reasoning behind distressing events and that we may gain a greater understanding as our spiritual knowledge develops, whether it be in this life or the next.

Religious Intolerance

The number of atrocities carried out in the name of religion is another impediment to belief in a God. Unfortunately, a very small minority of people, even smaller in modern times, have placed an interpretation on the Holy Writings that makes them feel justified in their barbaric activities. However, it is quite clear that any form of violence is contrary to the Golden Rule, and anyone inflicting harm on another has no mandate whatsoever to justify such actions on religious grounds. The vast majority of followers of all religions are totally against any form of violence, and those who act contrary to their own teachings will eventually be judged for their actions.

Religion and Science

The perceived conflict of religion and science is another reason that many reject religion. As scientific knowledge advances, many traditional spiritual teachings are judged to be contradictory. Unable to reconcile the religious teachings with scientific discoveries, people's tendency is often to reject the religion. Taking the aspect of human creation as an example, one could not accept both the literal story in the Bible and the scientific explanation of evolution. But if we treat the Bible story as a parable,[5] which is covered in more depth in part 2 of this book, we do not have to choose between the religious and the scientific explanations. Following the recent discovery of the Higgs boson, this particle has been referred to as the "God particle." The notion that this discovery somehow challenges the verity of the existence of a supernatural creator is absurd. It adds no more support to the absence of a creator than any other discovery, including the discovery of the existence of the universe itself. It is the line that might be followed by atheists, but believers who accept that science and religion can coexist would not see this

---

5 Parable: A narration of imagined events used to illustrate a moral or spiritual lesson.

latest discovery as any threat to their belief. Science is discovering the tools and method by which the universe was created as per the will of the Creator. In whatever way the universe was created, there is a scientific explanation. There is only one truth, so for religion and science to coexist, they must agree, as indeed they can and they do.

Life after Death; Heaven and Hell

Getting back to our original question—what happens to me when I die?—think of our previous short life in our mother's womb when we had no idea what was in store for us after birth. We were developing all the things that we would require—arms, legs, heart, lungs, ears, eyes, etc.—but we did not have the capacity to understand why. Similarly, if we are moving into a world that is far removed in its nature from our present world, we can only be guided by some assumptions and what we have been told by the prophets as far as what our next life will be like, despite the fact that we have developed some amazing thought processes of our own. Bear in mind that prophets rarely tell us anything that is beyond our capacity to comprehend, so the information we can glean from the writings of the prophets only gives us a glimpse of what we might expect.

It is not my intention to detail all the teachings of the prophets regarding our future spiritual realm. The religious teachings themselves are the best means of acquiring this information. If we were able to comprehend an existence where time does not exist or is irrelevant and where we can communicate with every person who has ever existed without the aid of any of the physical attributes that we use to communicate in our present life, we may have a smidgen of an idea of what awaits us. But realistically, we don't have that capacity.

The prophets speak of heaven and hell. In times past, because of mankind's limited maturity, these have been regarded more as physical places where we go when we die, with hell being portrayed as a horrible fiery place, whereas heaven was portrayed as a peaceful and happy place. Reincarnation is an aspect of heaven and hell that many people interpret as a physical transition, but there are many and varying interpretations as to the true meaning of reincarnation.

Now that we can envisage things in perhaps a more mature way, the more common understanding of heaven and hell is that these are states of spiritual existence that we will experience after leaving our present material life.

Another indication of the existence of an afterlife is the experience that many people have had when they were close to death or in fact when they had actually died but were brought back to life. These experiences have left many of these people with no doubt as to the existence of a world beyond, and they have no fears of dying as a result of their experience.

While none of this provides us with any scientific proof of a life after death and maybe that will always be the case, there are some fairly convincing reasons to believe that our life on earth is not our final form of existence. Furthermore, we are constantly reminded by the prophets that not only will our actions in this life affect our station or opportunities in the next life, but that our next life can be indescribably rewarding. So while we unwittingly developed the attributes for our present life before we were born, we should seriously consider the importance of developing the right spiritual attributes now, in preparation for our future eternal life.

CHAPTER 6

WHERE TO FROM HERE?

This book has so far has provided a perspective to unravel some of the confusion and remove some of the misconceptions that surround religion and spiritual matters. While it may not have explained God in a neat understandable package, we may gain some consolation in the fact that this is not possible. It is your own prerogative how you personalize or visualize that wonderful power we call God.

The following chapters in this book outline the basic history and framework of the religions that have been mentioned, as well as some brief references to some others. They do not go into great depth regarding the teachings of each religion, nor do they cover the various interpretations of the teachings, which are often not helpful if one is trying to get an overall perspective of each religion.

As the title of this book indicates, it is just a guide for beginners. We are all beginners when it comes to understanding God, so if we want to gain further knowledge on the subject, we should do this through further study and prayer.

Our search may have just begun. We should not give up on our quest. Its importance may have more significance than we can ever imagine, as it may well provide the foundation and the building blocks for our eternal future.

PART 2

REVELATION

CHAPTER 7

THE PROPHETS

Religion (the revelation of God's guidance) is certainly nothing new. In fact, it has been with us since mankind first had the capacity to think rationally and consider the existence of a higher power. As previously mentioned, there is wide recognition that knowledge of God and spiritual teachings have been revealed to mankind through a series of prophets or spiritual teachers. Many believe Adam to be the first man on earth and the first prophet or teacher to be illuminated with the Holy Spirit. He lived probably around six thousand years ago. The stories of Adam and Eve have fascinated mankind for thousands of years. The accounts of Adam and Eve as recorded in the Christian Bible, are often referred to as parables and therefore not necessarily treated as literal records of the events of the time, with the events in the Garden of Eden often regarded as a spiritual lesson about the forces of good and evil.

The followers of all the world's major religions hold their prophets in extremely high esteem, often to the extent of regarding them as God Himself. Certainly, it is only through the prophets and their teachings that we can gain a modicum of understanding about our Creator. Baha'u'llah, the prophet/founder of the Baha'i faith, describes the prophets as "Perfect Mirrors" in which the attributes of God are reflected.

There have been many well-known philosophers throughout history, such as Aristotle, Confucius and Guru Nanak, to name but a few, whose teachings have attracted large followings. These teachings have often been referred to as "religions" even though the authors of these teachings may never have claimed any divine source for their teachings. This doesn't mean that their teachings do not have validity.

Following is a chronology which includes a summary of the prophets whose teachings have been the foundation of some of the world's great religions. There are many thousands of spiritual movements that have sprung from these religions, some using additional teachings to those presented by the prophets, and everyone is free to study these and consider their merits.

Idris

Sabaeanism is one of the earliest recorded religions. Very little is known about the origins of this religion. Sabaeans claim to derive their religion from Seth and Idris.

It appears that the country where Sabaeanism became widespread was Chaldea, and Abraham is thought to have been a follower of that faith.

Idris has been mentioned in both the Qur'an, the Holy Book of Islam, and also by Baha'u'llah. The Qur'an states, "And commemorate Idrís in the Book; for he was a man of truth, a Prophet; And we uplifted him to a place on high." In Baha'u'llah's writings, He affirms, "The first person who devoted himself to philosophy was Idris. Thus was he named. Some called him also Hermes. In every tongue he hath a special name. He it is who hath set forth in every branch of philosophy thorough and convincing statements."

Krishna

The Bhagavad-Gita (Song of God) is universally renowned as the jewel of India's spiritual wisdom. Spoken by Lord Krishna to His intimate disciple Arjuna, the Gita's seven hundred concise verses provide a definitive guide to the science of self realization. It is considered the gospel of Hinduism. The essence of the teachings of Krishna is "that we should detach from materialism in order to evolve spiritually." No other philosophical or religious work reveals in such a lucid and profound way the nature of consciousness, the self, the universe, and the Supreme.

Indian as well as Western scholars have concluded that the period between 3200 and 3100 BCE is the period in which Lord Krishna lived on earth.

For generations, Krishna has been an enigma to some, but God to millions, who go ecstatic even as they hear His name. People consider Krishna their leader, hero, protector, philosopher, teacher, and friend all rolled into one. Krishna has influenced Indian thought, life, and culture in myriad ways. He has influenced not only its religion and philosophy, but also its mysticism and literature, painting and sculpture, dance, music, and all aspects of Indian folklore.

Many Hindus also use a series of books called the Vedas, which means "knowledge" in Sanskrit (the ancient language of the Hindus) and are thought to be some the world's oldest texts. Some Hindus believe the Vedas contains universal truth. There are four basic Vedic books. The Rig-Veda is the most important and contains mantras (hymns to the gods), which were composed thousands of years ago and were memorized, chanted, and passed down orally from one generation to the next before being written down in Sanskrit. The other Vedic books are Yajur-Veda, Sama-Veda, and Atharva-Veda.

Hinduism is indeed a fascinating religion. It is currently the world's third largest religion, after Christianity and Islam, and is the predominant and indigenous religion of the Indian subcontinent.

Abraham

Abraham is one of the central figures of the Jewish faith and also features prominently in the Christian and Islamic writings. According to Jewish tradition, Abraham was born under the name Abram in the city of Ur in Babylonia around 1800 BCE. He came to believe that the entire universe was the work of a single Creator, and he began to teach this belief to others. So it was Abraham that introduced the reality of monotheism (the belief in only one God), and this has been endorsed by the teachings of subsequent religions.

Abraham was raised as a city-dweller but adopted a nomadic lifestyle, traveling through what is now the land of Israel for many years.

According to both the Jewish Bible and the Qur'an, Abraham was the forefather of many tribes, including the Ishmaelites, Israelites, Midianites, Edomites, and others. Abraham was a descendant of Noah's son, Shem. Christians and Jews believe that Jesus is a descendant of Abraham, while Muslims believe that Muhammad was also a descendant through Ishmael.

Moses (circa 1392 BCE–1272 BCE)

Moses was born in Egypt, the son of Hebrew parents, Amram and Yochebe, at a time when the Pharaoh had ordered that all newborn male Hebrew children be cast into the Nile. He was rescued by the daughter of the Pharaoh. Having grown to adulthood, and aware of His Hebrew origin, and with deep compassion for His enslaved brethren, He became enraged while witnessing an Egyptian brutally beating a Hebrew slave. Impulsively, He killed the Egyptian. Fearing the Pharaoh's wrath and punishment, He fled into the desert of Midian, becoming a shepherd for Jethro, a Midianite priest, and later married Jethro's daughter, Zipporah. While tending the flocks on Mt. Horeb (Mt. Sinai) far in the wilderness, He beheld a bush burning that was not consumed. In the revelation that followed, He was informed that He had been chosen to serve as the liberator of the children of Israel. He was also told to proclaim the unity of God to His entire people, a doctrine which had previously been known to a small number of people.

Moses returned to Egypt and persuaded the Hebrews to organize for a hasty departure from the land of bondage. Together with His brother, Aaron, He informed the Pharaoh that the God of the Hebrews demanded that He free His people. The Pharaoh initially refused this demand, but following a series of events wrought upon Egypt by the power invested in Moses by God, the Pharaoh granted the Hebrews permission to depart immediately. Moses thus found himself the leader of an undisciplined collection of slaves, Hebrew as well as non-Hebrew, escaping from Egyptian territory to freedom.

Moses' immediate goal was Mt. Horeb, called Mt. Sinai, where God had first revealed Himself to Moses. The Hebrews came to the sacred mountain fired by the inspiration of their prophetic leader. Summoned by God, Moses ascended the mountain and received the tablets of stone inscribed with the Ten Commandments. Inspired, the people agreed to the conditions of the Covenant.

Throughout forty years in the wilderness of Sinai, Moses overcame tremendous obstacles and shaped His people into a nation. He molded the former slaves into a people with the highest ethical standards.

Moses supplemented the Ten Commandments by a code of laws regulating the social and religious life of His people. This collection of instructions, read to and ratified by the people, was called the Book of the Covenant.

The religion of Moses was known as Judaism, and the Holy Book was known as the Torah, which also formed the first five books of the Christian Bible: Genesis, Exodus, Numbers, Leviticus, and Deuteronomy. The Tanakh or Written Torah refers to the whole body of Jewish law and teachings.

Today, about 42 per cent of all Jews reside in Israel and about 42 per cent reside in the United States and Canada, with most of the remainder living in Europe.

The Ten Commandments, as well as other traditions and texts from Judaism, have been endorsed by subsequent prophets, (Jesus, Muhammad, The Bab, and Baha'u'llah) and have become a foundation for the code of laws of many societies, so I felt it appropriate to list them here. More recent translations have modified some of the Old English style of the wording.

The Ten Commandments (Exodus 20)

1. Thou shalt have no other gods before me.
2. Thou shalt not make unto thee any graven image, or any likeness of anything that is in heaven above, or that is in the earth beneath, or that is in the water under the earth: Thou shalt not bow down thyself to them, nor serve them: for I the LORD thy God am a jealous God, visiting the iniquity of the fathers upon the children unto the third and fourth generation of them that hate me; And shewing mercy unto thousands of them that love me, and keep my commandments.
3. Thou shalt not take the name of the LORD thy God in vain; for the LORD will not hold him guiltless that taketh His name in vain.
4. Remember the Sabbath day, to keep it holy. Six days shalt thou labor, and do all thy work. But the seventh day is the Sabbath of the LORD thy God. In it thou shalt not do any work, thou, nor thy son, nor thy daughter, thy manservant, nor thy maidservant, nor thy cattle, nor thy stranger that is within thy gates. For in six days the LORD made heaven and earth, the sea, and all that in them is, and rested the seventh day; wherefore the LORD blessed the Sabbath day, and hallowed it.

5. Honor thy father and thy mother that thy days may be long upon the land which the LORD thy God giveth thee.
6. Thou shalt not kill.
7. Thou shalt not commit adultery.
8. Thou shalt not steal.
9. Thou shalt not bear false witness against thy neighbor.
10. Thou shalt not covet thy neighbor's house; thou shalt not covet thy neighbor's wife, nor his manservant, nor his maidservant, nor his ox, nor his ass, nor any thing that is thy neighbor's.

Zoroaster

Zoroaster, also known as Zarathustra, was born in Azerbaijan in Northern Persia, and although there are conflicting reports of the period of His ministry, it appears that it was probably around 660 BCE. It is thought that He lived to about seventy-seven years of age.

Zoroaster proclaimed that man has choice, and that his choice for good over evil is the voice of his own destiny, in accordance with the will of God. A good choice is a choice for the good, which assures one's destiny in the afterlife. Zoroaster inspired confidence that the reign of righteousness would ultimately triumph over evil at the end of time.

From a Christian perspective, the Three Wise Men who reportedly visited Jesus at the time of His birth were thought to be followers of Zoroaster. Also, Christian teachings had much in common with the teachings of Zoroaster, as in fact had many of the great religions.

A significant number of Zoroastrians converted to the Baha'i faith in the latter half of the nineteenth century, mainly those from Yazd and Kerman, believing Baha'u'llah to be the promised Sháh Bahrám Varjávand, a Zoroastrian messianic king foretold in several Persian texts.

Zoroaster's birthday is celebrated on March 21 each year as part of the Persian New Year Festival.

Buddha (Siddhārtha Gautama Buddha)

Buddha was reputed to have been born in Lumbini, in Northern India, now Nepal. The Buddhist religion is prominent throughout most of Asia.

The time of Buddha's birth and death are uncertain, however most early twentieth-century historians dated His lifetime as around 563 BCE to 483 BCE. Some more recent opinion dates His death as late as 400 BCE. The title of "Buddha" means "Enlightened One."

There are many branches of Buddhism, and Buddhists have differing views on the existence of a higher power. This is understandable as Buddha appeared to make little reference to such a power. Perhaps the closest reference to this would be the following from the Buddhist writings:

> "There is O monks, an Unborn, Unoriginated, Uncreated, Unformed. Were there not, O monks, this Unborn, Unoriginated, Uncreated, Unformed, there would be no escape from the world of the born, originated, created, formed."(Udana, 80-81)

When Buddha was asked questions regarding the existence of a higher power, He would not give a straight answer. Sometimes He would imply that the answer was "neither knowable nor unknowable," and that spending lots of time and argument trying to find an answer was therefore "not conducive to spiritual life."

The question then arises: Who do Buddhists pray to?

For Buddhists, prayer is a practice to awaken inherent inner capacities of strength, compassion, and wisdom. It is a form of meditation; it is a practice of inner reconditioning. Many Buddhists therefore believe that this higher power is within ourselves.

Is this necessarily contrary to the beliefs of other religions?

For believers, it is generally recognized that God is beyond words, beyond thought, and beyond description. It is also an accepted belief that God is omnipresent (present everywhere at the same time), so it should not be an issue to accept that God is within us.

As soon as you put a label on God, it personalizes this amazing power and tends to give it time and space. Could it be that Buddha wanted to avoid this? It is impossible for mankind in the twenty-first century to comprehend God, so how much more difficult would it have been for those living 2,500 years ago to have dealt with such a concept?

The teachings of Buddha were very much aimed at making people aware of spiritual values, rather than focusing on the material things of life. The goal of all true Buddhists is Nirvana (enlightenment), which is the supreme state free from suffering and individual existence.

Nothing here conflicts with the teachings of any of the other religions. The belief in life after death is also something that Buddhism has in common with other faiths.

People who are intent on denigrating certain religions as being false often raise the Buddhist belief in reincarnation as a major point of difference, and they often put their own uninformed interpretation on the meaning of reincarnation. There are many variations on the understanding of the writings on this topic, and indeed, many teachings on this subject were inherited from religious teachings prior to the time of Buddha, which may well have been misinterpreted as they were handed down over many hundreds of years. However, in Buddhism there is a concept of *annata* (no self), so it is not the self of the person that returns but the collection of the five *khandhas*, the predispositions and characteristics of an individual.

One thing that is clear in Buddhist teachings is the concept of progressive revelation. Buddha said:

I am not the first Buddha Who came upon this earth, nor shall I be the last. In due time another Buddha will arise in the world, a Holy One, a supremely enlightened One, endowed with wisdom in conduct, auspicious knowing the universe, an incomparable leader of men, a Master of angels and mortals. He will reveal to you the same eternal truths which I have taught you. He will preach to you His religion, glorious in its origin, glorious at the climax and glorious at the goal, in spirit and in the letter. He will proclaim a religious life, wholly perfect and pure, such as I now proclaim. His disciples will number many thousands, while Mine number many hundreds. (According to the Gospel of Buddha by Carus p. 217 & 218)

Jesus

Jesus, usually referred to as Jesus Christ, was born in Palestine, now Israel. The word "Christ" means anointed or baptized. A significant episode in the life of Jesus was His anointing by John the Baptist. Whilst, like all of the world's major religions, Christianity had its roots in the East, Christianity is the religion that became widespread in the Western world and is the predominant religion in most English speaking countries. The book of the Christians is the Holy Bible. First produced some four hundred years after the time of Jesus, it is a compilation of scriptures from various sources, the main ones being the writings of four apostles named Matthew, Mark, Luke, and John. Their writings form the first four chapters, or books, of the New Testament of the Holy Bible. The Old Testament relates to the time before Jesus, whereas the New Testament mainly covers the time during the life of Jesus and the teachings that He gave us. These teachings form the basis of Christianity.

Despite the production of the Bible many centuries after the time of Jesus, Christians believe it to be an accurate record of events. Any disagreements regarding the accuracy of the Bible pale into insignificance in comparison to the wonderful teachings provided to us as recorded in the Bible. Christianity forms a continuation of the teachings of Moses, and a strong foundation of Christian ethics is the Ten Commandments given to Moses by God.

Much of the mystique of Christianity revolves around the birth and the death of Jesus, and Christians place much emphasis on these events as a means of demonstrating the divine station of Jesus. Christian belief is that Mary, the mother of Jesus, was a virgin, and that Jesus, rather than having a human father, was the Son of God. Because of His claims, which raised the ire of many of the Jews and the governing Romans, Jesus was killed. He was crucified (hung on a cross), and Christians believe that He was resurrected and appeared to His disciples. This followed stories of finding empty the tomb in which He had been placed. There is a lot of disagreement around the true meaning of the story of the Resurrection, and this is one of the reasons that the Christian church has suffered so much fragmentation. These man-made divisions, however, do not detract from the quality of Jesus' teachings, which two thousand years later, still form the basis for the legal system and the moral code by which we live our lives, particularly in the Western world.

Muhammad (570–632 CE)

Muhammad was born in the town of Mecca in the desert of Western Arabia. In His early life, He worked as a shepherd and a merchant and became well known for His honesty. At the age of twenty-five He married a wealthy Meccan merchant named Khadija, who was some twenty years His senior. They had six children; however, His two sons died in infancy.

The fascinating life history of Muhammad is more comprehensively documented than that of Jesus or the earlier prophets, and a study of this provides us with a good understanding of the conditions that prevailed in the Middle East during this time.

Muhammad's first revelation from God came when He was about forty years of age. It is recorded that He was terrified by this experience but was consoled by His wife, Khadija.

After several similar experiences, Muhammad began to reveal to His tribe the messages He was receiving. These messages were saved and later would become the Qur'an, Islam's sacred scripture.

Muhammad confirmed the validity of the prophets of the past and proclaimed new teachings appropriate for His people. He introduced many new laws that formed the basis of Islamic Law, which continues to be observed by Moslems.

One of Muhammad's main missions was to unite the warring tribes of Arabia, and He did this very successfully through His teachings. Yet He never sought power for Himself. He said, "I am nothing but a warner and a herald of glad tidings unto people who will believe" (The Qur'an 7:188).

He explained the meaning of the original teachings of Adam and Abraham, which had been misinterpreted or corrupted over time.

The Islamic religion, based on teachings of Muhammad, is the predominant religion of the Middle East and is experiencing significant growth worldwide.

The Bab (1819–1850 CE)

Perhaps the least known of the major religions is the Babi faith. This is because the prophet/founder of the faith, Siyyid 'Ali-Muhammad (later known as The Bab, meaning "the gate") had a very short ministry of just six years. Nevertheless, the Bab's influence at the time of His declaration in 1844 in Shiraz, Persia, was immediate and tumultuous. Such was the growth of His following that the Moslem clergy of the time became extremely nervous and had Him executed along with many thousands of His followers. The events surrounding The Bab's execution were truly remarkable, producing an amazing spectacle, and these events were well-documented in the newspapers of the day as well as forming part of the history of the Babi and Baha'i faiths.

The teachings of the Bab are contained in the Bayan and focus strongly on the fact that His coming ushered in the "age of fulfilment." However, the Bab, while proclaiming Himself as a Manifestation of God, said that His main mission was to prepare the way for one far greater than Himself.

Baha'u'llah (1817–1892 CE)

Mirza Husayn 'Ali, who later assumed the title of Baha'u'llah (meaning the "Glory of God"), was born in Mazindaran, Persia, in 1817. His noble family could trace its lineage to the ruling dynasties of Persia's imperial past and was endowed with wealth and vast estates. Turning His back on a position at court, which these advantages offered Him, Bahá'u'lláh became known for His generosity and kindliness which made Him deeply loved among His countrymen.

In 1863, He openly declared that He was the one foretold by The Bab and through voluminous writings has provided spiritual guidance for a rapidly changing and modern world. A study of the Bab's writings provides strong evidence of the validity of Baha'u'llah's claim.

Baha'u'llah proclaimed that His coming fulfilled the prophecies of the religions of the past, and followers of many religions have become Baha'is on the strength of accepting these claims.

He proclaimed the Oneness of God, that all religions come from the same source, that mankind should regarded as one family, the need for the removal of all forms of prejudice, the importance of the independent investigation of truth, the need for an international auxiliary language, the equality of men and women, the importance of a basic education for all, that science and religion must agree, the need for the abolition of extremes of wealth and poverty, the requirement for a world federation to resolve international disputes, and the importance of the preservation of cultural diversity.

Baha'u'llah's teachings clearly enunciate the fact that God has never left mankind without guidance, which has been provided by a series of prophets, and that this "Ancient Covenant" would continue.

However, He made it quite clear that there would not be another prophet until the expiration of a full thousand years.

Baha'u'llah's claims and radical teachings raised the ire of the clergy, and as a result He spent much of His life either in prison or under house arrest. Much of His time in prison was spent enduring atrocious conditions. He was also banished from city to city in the hope of diminishing His following.

While in Adrianople, Bahá'u'lláh addressed tablets to the kings and rulers of the world asking them to accept His revelation, renounce their material possessions, work together to settle disputes, and endeavor toward the betterment of the world and its peoples. He urged them to rule with justice and protect the rights of the downtrodden. He also told the rulers to reduce their armaments and reconcile their differences. The Christian monarchs were also asked to be faithful to Jesus' call to follow the promised "Spirit of Truth."

The failure of most of the world leaders to respond to Baha'u'llah's call coincided with the downfall of many of these leaders at a time they had immense power, an aspect of history that has perplexed many historians.

As with the advent of the religions of the past, there was no widespread acceptance of Baha'u'llah by any religious group, and the patterns of the past were repeated, with the teachings being spread initially by a relatively small number of believers, most of whom were followers of the Bab. However, with modern-day improvements in communication, the growth of the Baha'i faith has experienced a much faster growth than the other major religions experienced in their early days.

Unlike many of the prophets of the past, many of Baha'u'llah's teachings are written by His own hand, thereby avoiding misunderstanding. He also clearly defined the future authority for the faith that He introduced, thus ensuring its security and avoiding future schisms.

Baha'u'llah was descended from Zoroaster and the Sasaniyan kings of Persia, thereby fulfilling certain traditions that the great Redeemer of mankind would be of pure Persian lineage. Baha'u'llah was also descended from Abraham through Abraham's third wife, Katurah, thus uniting in His own person two branches of the Aryan religions[6] and the Semitic religions.[7]

---

6 Aryan religions: Religions that originated among the Aryans, a powerful group of Indo-European-speaking people who spread through Iran and northern India around 1500 to 2000 BCE. Later in their history, the Aryans were influenced by several other religions, including Hinduism and Buddhism. The Indo-Aryan Vedas are the oldest scriptures of Hinduism, and thereby Hinduism was influenced by Aryan religious teachings.
7 Semitic religions: The Semitic religions are those that developed among the Semites, descendants of Shem, the son of Noah. Major Semitic religions are Judaism, Christianity, and Islam.

CHAPTER 8

THE ENIGMA OF THE FULFILMENT OF PROPHECY

Even though many religions have experienced widespread euphoria regarding the fulfilment of the prophecies of their own prophets and this expectation has often been pinpointed at a specific, future period in time, the period passes with little more than a handful of people acknowledging that any such event took place.

A prime example of this is the intense expectation by the Jewish people around the time of Jesus regarding the coming of the Messiah. While to future theologians, and certainly Christians, the fact that Jesus fulfilled many prophecies from Jewish scriptures is a crystal clear reality, but because the Jews at the time of Jesus had a very clear understanding that the Messiah would come "with a sword," they did not accept Jesus and in fact Jews appeared to play a major role in the events that led to His crucifixion. There is a strong school of thought that many prophecies contained in the Torah refer to a much later time in history, because events that were prophesied as preceding the coming of the Messiah had not yet come to pass at the time of Jesus.

Similarly, many Christians and Moslems, past and present, have had equally strong convictions regarding the fulfilment of the prophecies of their own prophet. This expectation was never stronger that if was in the middle of the nineteenth century. In fact, this period saw the introduction of many new religious movements. It was precisely at this time that the Bab, closely followed by Baha'u'llah, declared their stations and the fact that the "Promise of All Ages" had come.

Although Abraham introduced monotheism nearly four thousand years ago and this concept of "a single God but many prophets" is accepted by all the followers of the major religions in respect to the previous prophets, the recognition of a new prophet is not something that happens as a matter of course. There are literally millions of followers of many religions awaiting the fulfilment of the prophecies of their own religion, and each one of them believes that it will be obvious when such an event occurs, even though it has never been obvious in the past.

Speaking about His own return, Jesus said He would come "like a thief in the night." (Thessalonians 5:2-4). A thief does not preannounce the time of his arrival, and usually the event is not noticed until he is gone.

So, for those awaiting an announcement to be flashed across our television screens, broadcast on our radios, texted to us on our cell phones, and endorsed by all the religious leaders of the day, forget it—it will never happen that way.

Chapter 9

Focus on the Positive

The interpretations of various passages in the teachings of the prophets, mainly with regard to the ongoing direction and authority of the religion, have led to significant splits. A prime example of this is the splitting of the Christian church into Catholicism and Protestantism. Also, varying interpretation of the scriptures regarding the teachings of Jesus have resulted in many different sects of Christianity being established, and each of these sects has adopted its own interpretation on the prophecies, particularly with regard to the return of Christ. And it is not only Christianity that has broken into schisms. The Islamic faith has also suffered a major split into Sunni Islam and Shia Islam. Similar divisions have occurred in many religions, all as a result of differing interpretations. Focusing on these divisions is not helpful. It detracts from the beauty and quality of the teachings, so readers are encouraged to focus on the aspects of religion that unites people rather than those that cause division.

Also, it is important to differentiate between culture and religion. While each religion has been revealed to people of different cultures, it is important that we don't judge a religion based on the culture of the people that follow that religion. While one of the fascinating aspects of travel and closer communication is the knowledge we gain of the different cultures, there may be some things we find strange, sometimes objectionable, and it is an easy trap to fall into to associate the activity with the religion of those people, whereas it may have nothing at all to do with the religion. It may be something that has arisen out of a misinterpretation of a religious teaching, but often it is a cultural thing which has no religious base whatsoever. We could provide many examples of this in all of the religions, but as many people are very protective of their cultural practices, we will refrain from doing so. The passage of time, the sharing of opinions and improved education will tend to minimize some less acceptable customs, while the positive and more spiritually based customs will flourish and enhance the overall quality of the global society.

There is a huge amount of material available for those who wish to study religion in greater depth. However, it is important to choose your information sources carefully, as many publications and websites are created for the purpose of denigrating certain religions, and often contain many untruths and quote things out of context. You will find conflicting views on many aspects of religion, including variations in timeframes and names of historical figures, and this is understandable as much religious history has been handed down by word of mouth over many thousands of years.

Nevertheless, there is a wealth of information in all the religions that link them all together and demonstrate an overwhelming similarity in the spiritual teachings of all the religions. So look past the differences, and enjoy the beauty and value of the spiritual teachings that God has provided to us since time immemorial. The study of religion throughout history with an open mind is fascinating as it provides the student with both an amazing knowledge of history and a wealth of invaluable spiritual guidance and insight.

Religion is alive! It's the language of God. Enjoy it.

REFERENCES

Note: All definitions are taken from *The Concise Oxford Dictionary*. Fowler, (H.W. Fowler, F.G. Fowler, and David Crystal. 11th edition. Oxford: Oxford University Press, 2011).